RP

W9-BPN-084

How an
Egg Grows Into
a Chicken

Written by
Tanya Kant

Illustrated by
Carolyn Franklin

Crack!

Hold the page
up to the light
to see the chick
inside the egg.

children's press®
An Imprint of Scholastic Inc.
NEW YORK • TORONTO • LONDON • AUCKLAND • SYDNEY
MEXICO CITY • NEW DELHI • HONG KONG
DANBURY, CONNECTICUT

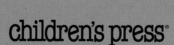

© The Salariya Book Company Ltd MMVIII
No part of this publication may be reproduced in whole or in part, or stored in a retrieval system, or transmitted in any form or by any means, electronic, mechanical, photocopying, recording, or otherwise, without written permission of the copyright holder. For information regarding permission, write to salariya@salariya.com

Published in Great Britain in 2008 by
The Salariya Book Company Ltd
25 Marlborough Place, Brighton BN1 1UB
England
www.salariya.com
ISBN-13: 978-0-531-24047-2 (lib. bdg.) 978-0-531-23801-1 (pbk.)
ISBN-10: 0-531-24047-9 (lib. bdg.)   0-531-23801-6 (pbk.)
All rights reserved.
Published in 2009 in the United States
by Children's Press
An imprint of Scholastic Inc.

A CIP catalog record for this book is available
from the Library of Congress.

Author: **Tanya Kant** is a graduate of the University of Sussex at Brighton, England. She specializes in writing and editing children's nonfiction, and is especially interested in natural science and history. She lives in Hove, England.

Artist: **Carolyn Franklin** graduated from Brighton College of Art with a focus on design and illustration. Since then she has worked in animation, advertising, and children's fiction and nonfiction. She has a special interest in natural history and has written many books on the subject, including *Life in the Wetlands* in the **WHAT ON EARTH?** series and *Egg to Owl* in the **CYCLES OF LIFE** series.

Consultant: **Monica Hughes** is an experienced educational advisor and author of more than one hundred books for young children. She has been head teacher of a primary school, primary advisory teacher, and senior lecturer in early childhood education.

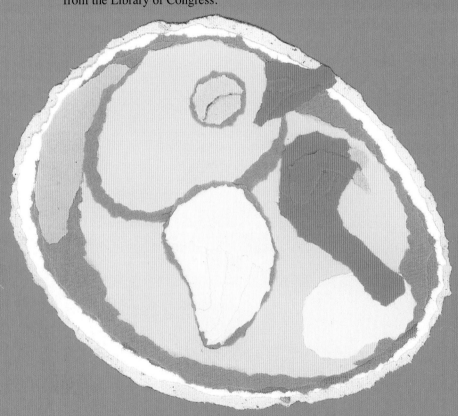

Printed and bound in China.

PAPER FROM
SUSTAINABLE
FORESTS

Contents

What Is a Chicken?

A chicken is a bird. All birds have feathers, a beak, and a pair of wings. A female chicken is called a **hen** and a male chicken is called a **rooster**. Baby chickens are called **chicks**. All chickens begin life in an egg.

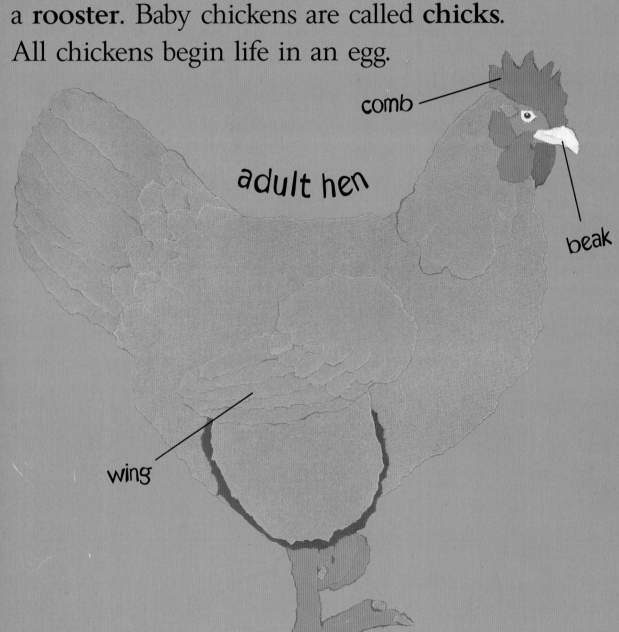

comb

adult hen

beak

wing

comb

beak

wattle

adult rooster

wing

5

Why Do Hens Build Nests?

All hens lay eggs. Before a hen lays her eggs, she builds a soft, warm **nest** to keep them safe. She uses straw to make the nest, and lines it with her own soft feathers.

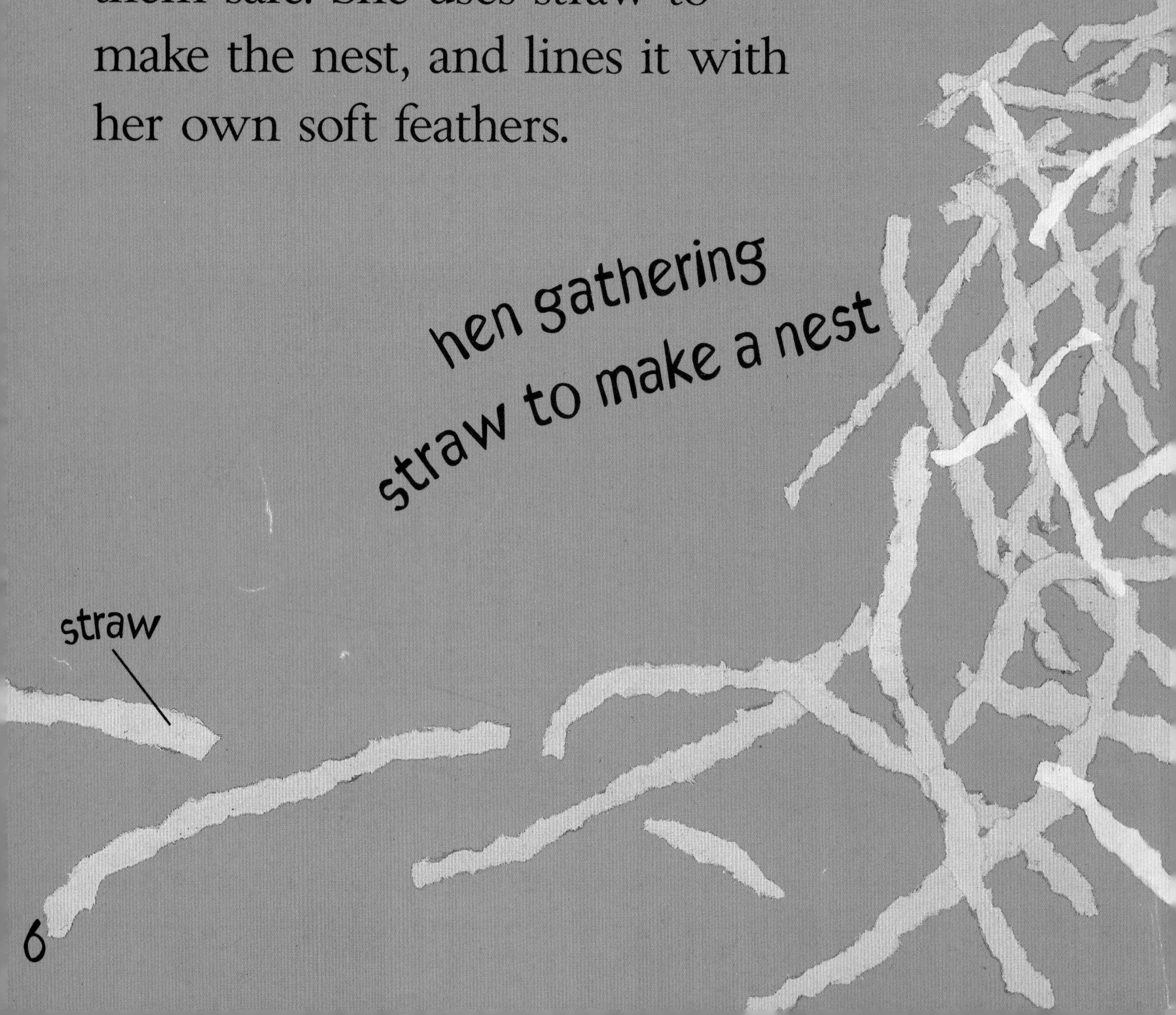

hen gathering straw to make a nest

straw

6

Once the nest is built, the hen can lay
her eggs. She lays one or two eggs a
day until she has about twelve.

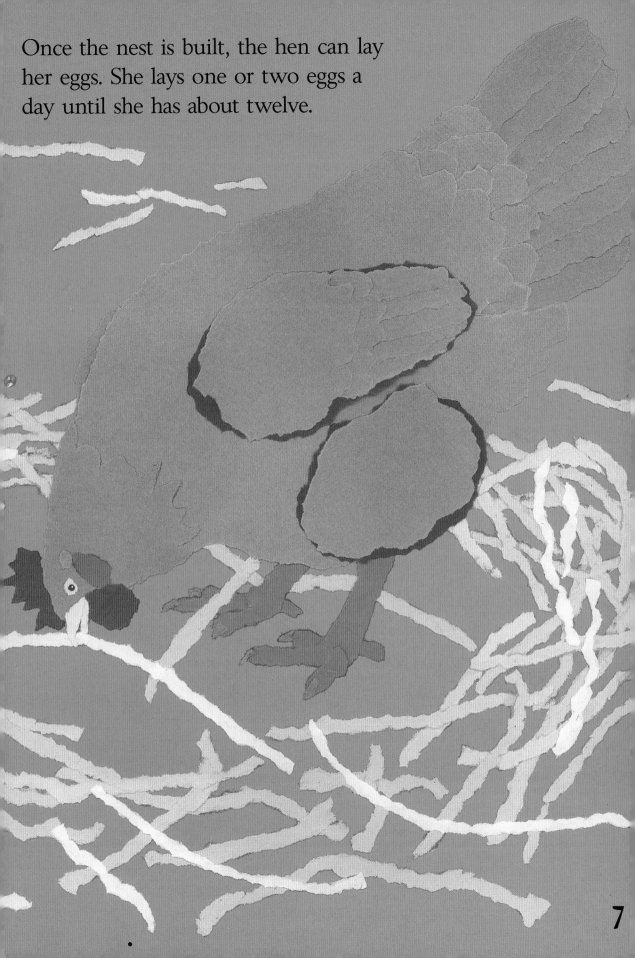

What Is Inside an Egg?

A hen's eggs are **fertilized** when the hen and rooster **mate**. An egg will hatch into a chicken only if it has been fertilized. Each fertilized egg holds and protects something that will grow into a baby bird.

The eggs that we eat are not fertilized. They do not have a baby bird inside.

eggs

8

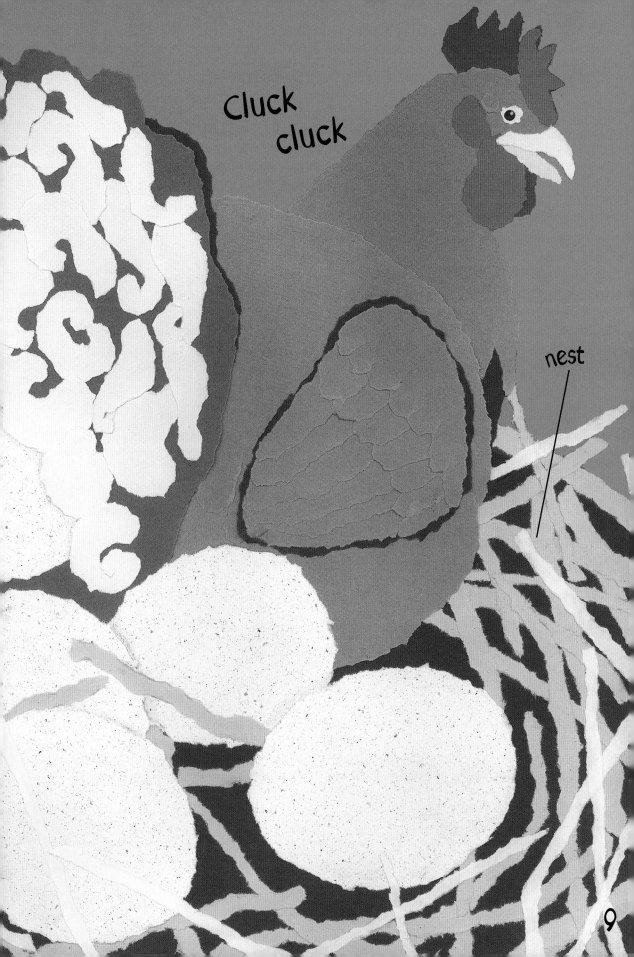

Cluck
cluck

nest

9

How Does the Chick Grow Inside the Egg?

At first the young chick inside the egg is just a tiny dot called an **embryo**. As the embryo grows, it slowly begins to look like a bird.

The egg also contains yellow **yolk**. The baby chick feeds on the yolk, which helps it to grow.

The embryo and yolk lie in egg white or **albumen**. This jelly-like substance protects the embryo and helps it grow.

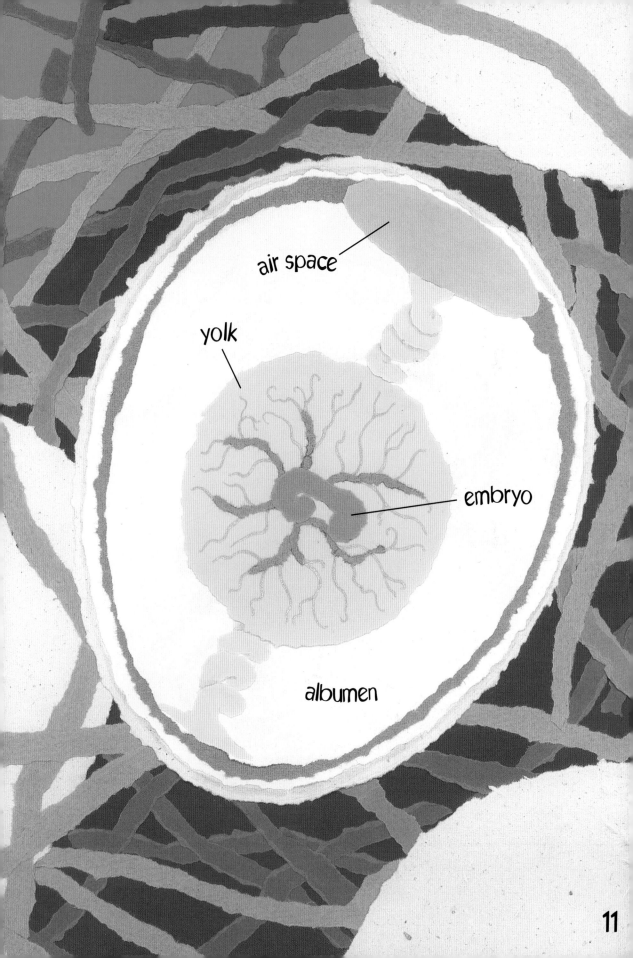

Why Does a Hen Sit on Her Eggs?

A hen sits on her eggs to keep them warm. This is called **brooding**. The eggs don't break because their shells are strong and hard.

soft feathers

The mother hen surrounds the eggs with her soft feathers. Every now and then she turns the eggs to keep them warm all over.

cluck
cluck

The hen calls to her chicks.

When Does the Egg Hatch?

After 21 days, the baby chick inside the egg starts to make a cheeping noise. This lets the hen know that her chicks are about to **hatch**. The hen makes a clucking sound to encourage them to come out. All of the eggs will hatch at around the same time.

Hold this page up to the light to see the chicks hatch.

Soon the eggshells begin to crack.

Crack!

Cheep
cheep

wet chick

egg tooth

How Does the Chick Break Free From Its Egg?

The chick has a little point on its beak which is called an **egg tooth**. It uses this to make a hole in the eggshell from the inside. It takes a few hours for the chick to break free. When it first hatches, the chick is wet and slimy all over. The chick soon dries out and looks like a fluffy, round ball.

Cheep
cheep
cheep

What Do Chicks Eat?

Even very young chicks eat the same foods as their mother. They **peck** and scratch at the ground, looking for grains, seeds, and grubs. The chicks make cheeping sounds all the time so their mother knows where they are.

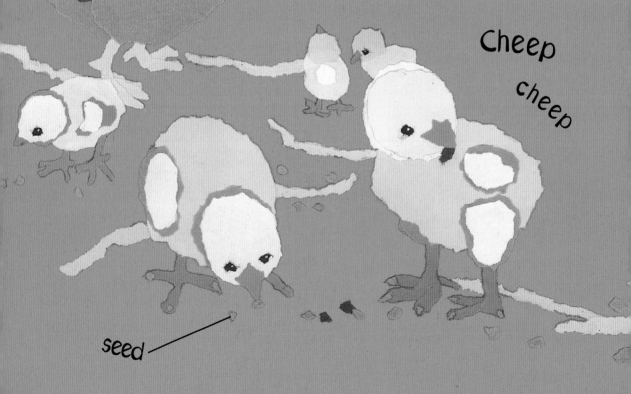

hen

Cheep cheep

seed

grain

Chicks peck and wander.

At first the chicks follow
their mother. As they get
older, they start to explore
their new surroundings.

The fluffy chick grows.

grub

When Does a Chick Start to Look Like a Chicken?

As the chick gets older, new feathers start to grow. In a few months, the chick will lose its fluffy yellow feathers and grow silky brown adult ones. A young hen is ready to lay her first eggs when she is about 25 weeks old.

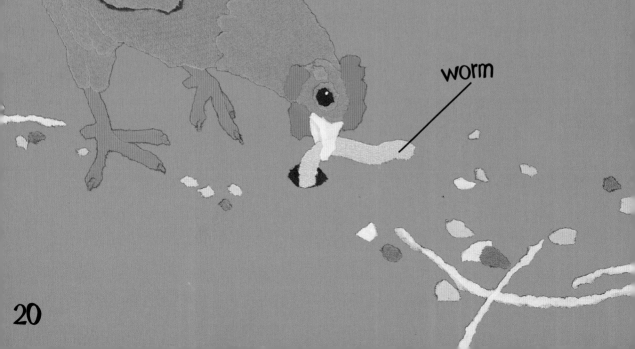

worm

bright red
comb

A **bantam** is a kind of chicken
that does not grow very big.

bantam chicken

21

What Animals Like to Eat Chicken Eggs?

Birds, foxes, lizards, and snakes all like to eat eggs. To get at the food inside, some animals bite or peck at the eggshell. Others smash it with stones. Snakes like to swallow eggs whole!

Squawk!

hungry fox

hen protecting
her eggs

The hen tries to
protect her eggs.
She flaps her wings
and makes noises to
scare the fox away.

Why Do Humans Keep Chickens?

Humans keep chickens for their eggs and meat. They are often kept on farms, in barns, or in specially built shelters called **coops**.

Cheep cheep

A group of chickens is called a **flock**. Flocks are usually made up of just hens and their chicks. Sometimes a flock has a rooster, too.

Cluck

cluck

25

Chicken Facts

Wild chickens live in the tropical forests of Asia, Africa, and South America. They are called jungle fowl.

A good laying hen will lay 250 to 300 eggs a year.

Young hens often lay eggs that have two yolks.

Eggs are stronger than you think. A typical chicken egg will support a weight of nearly 9 pounds before breaking.

An average chicken weighing 5½ pounds has a wingspan of around 33 inches.

A frizzle is a type of chicken
with curly feathers. Silkies
have very soft, fluffy
feathers.

The White Sully is said to be
the biggest and heaviest breed
of chicken. The Serama
bantam from Southeast Asia
is said to be the smallest.

Cluck
cluck

Cheep
cheep

27

Things to Do

How strong is an egg?

Ask an adult to help you with these experiments!

Do this experiment over a sink, just in case you make a mistake. Place an egg in the palm of your hand. Close your hand so that your fingers are completely wrapped around the egg. Squeeze the egg by applying even pressure all around the shell.

If you do it correctly, the egg will not break. This is because the pressure from your fingers is spread all over the surface of the egg.

It's easy to crack an egg on the side of a bowl, because the pressure is all on one side of the egg.

The floating egg

1. Put a raw egg in a cup of water. Does the egg float or sink?

2. It should sink— unless it's old. (Older eggs have pockets of air in them.)

3. Add 8 tablespoons of salt to the water and stir. What happens now?

4. Stirring makes the salt dissolve into the water. The added salt makes the water more dense than the egg. The egg will now float above the denser salt water.

Life Cycle of a Chicken

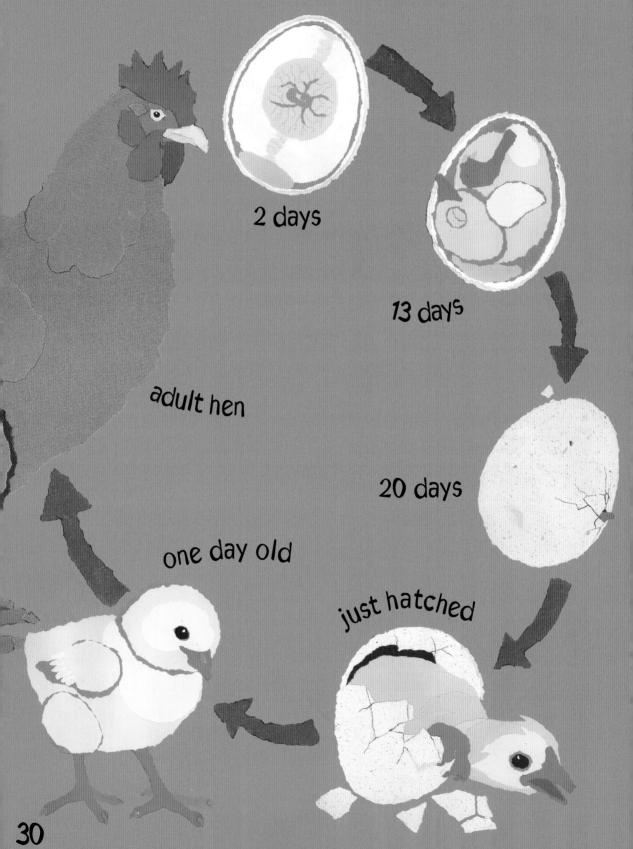

2 days

13 days

adult hen

20 days

one day old

just hatched

Words to Remember

Albumen The clear, jelly-like substance inside an egg that protects the embryo and the yolk. It is also called egg white.

Bantam A small type of chicken.

Brood To sit on eggs to keep them warm.

Chick A baby chicken.

Coop A shelter for chickens.

Egg tooth A little point on the tip of a chick's beak that helps it to break the shell of its egg.

Embryo The first stage in the growth of the chicken inside the egg.

Fertilized egg An egg laid by a hen that has mated with a rooster. A chick can grow only in a fertilized egg.

Flock A group of chickens.

Hatch To break out of an egg.

Hen An adult female chicken.

Mate To join together to make a baby animal.

Nest A safe place made by the hen for laying her eggs.

Peck To jab at or bite with the beak.

Rooster An adult male chicken.

Wattle A loose piece of skin that hangs from the neck of an adult chicken.

Yolk The yellow substance inside an egg that feeds the embryo.

Index